PAPER CRAFTS

By Linda Hetzer

Photographs by Steven Mays

Raintree

Milwaukee • Toronto • Melbourne • London

PROJECT DESIGNS: Rubbings, Wendy Davidson

PRODUCTION: Designer, Deborah Bracken
            Illustrators, Lynn Matus and Sally Shimizu
            Text editor, Jill Munves

Library of Congress Number: 77-28796

1 2 3 4 5 6 7 8 9 0 82 81 80 79 78

Printed and bound in the United States of America.

Library of Congress Cataloging in Publication Data

Hetzer, Linda.
    Paper crafts.

    SUMMARY: Introduces various techniques in block
printing, rubbings, and papermaking. Includes step-by-
step instructions for a selection of projects involving each craft.
    1. Rubbing — Juvenile literature. 2. Paper making
and trade — Juvenile literature. 3. Relief printing —
Juvenile literature. [1. Rubbing. 2. Paper making
and trade. 3. Relief printing. 4. Handicraft]
I. Mays, Steven. II. Shimizu, Sally. III. Matus, Lynn.
IV. Title.
TT912.H47 745.54   77-28796
ISBN 0-8172-1186-1

SYMBOLS

The symbols that appear near the title of each project tell several things at a glance: how difficult the project is, about how much time it takes to finish it, and the kind of materials you need to make it.

Complexity

Easy

Average

Challenging

Time

One hour

One afternoon

Several days

Materials

Found objects
(things you have around the house)

Variety store items

Special craft tools or materials

CONTENTS

BLOCK PRINTING

Block printing can be done with wood, linoleum, potatoes, or rubber stamps. The materials may be different, but the blocks have a similarity. The design on every block is made up of two types of areas – the area that is cut away and the area that is left standing. The area left standing is the area that picks up the paint or ink. And when pressed on a piece of paper, it is the area that prints. The advantage of block printing is that one block can be used over and over again to print the same design.

Long before the invention of the printing press, books were printed with blocks. The words and pictures for each page were carved from a block of wood. The blocks were then inked and pressed against the pages. And the pages were bound together to form a book.

Most blocks are carved, with some areas being cut away. But blocks can also be built up in layers. For example, you can glue pieces of cardboard on top of each other. Whatever is on the highest layer will pick up the ink and print.

MATERIALS

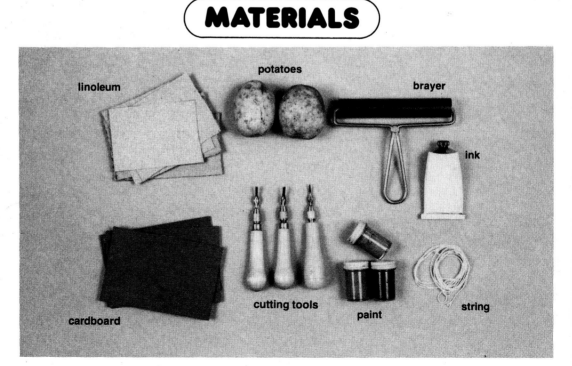

linoleum · potatoes · brayer · ink · cardboard · cutting tools · paint · string

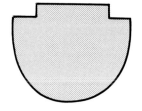

Vegetable prints

A great variety of vegetables can be used to make vegetable prints. You can try potatoes, cucumbers, carrots, celery, squash, peppers, parsnips, and zucchini. Soft vegetables, such as tomatoes, are not good for printing, but any vegetable that is firm enough to hold its shape when it is cut can be used. In addition to the vegetables, you will need tempera paint and lots of paper.

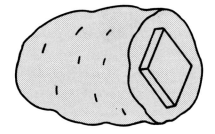

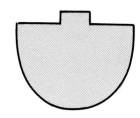

1 Cut the cucumber and other long vegetables into 2-in. (5-cm) pieces. Cut the potatoes in half. Most of the vegetables can be used just as you cut them, but the potatoes need some extra work.

2 On the surface of the potato, carve out a design. Have an adult help you with this. As you work, leave the part that is to print raised, but cut away the area around it. In the top drawing above, a potato with a square is shown. The picture below it shows how the potato looks from the side. As shown in the next two drawings, you can also cut shapes like rectangles and stripes into potatoes.

3 Dip the cut vegetables into the tempera paint. (The cucumber will print the design of its seeds. It does not need to be carved.)

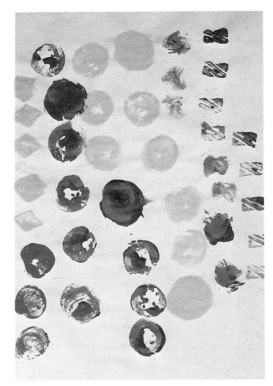

4 Press the paint-covered surface of the vegetable on the paper. You can make several prints before you have to dip the vegetable into the paint again.

You can use many vegetables and different colors of paint to make your design.

Packing-foam prints

Packing foam is a type of plastic that is used for packing. It is put around a radio, for example, so the radio can be shipped in a cardboard carton without being damaged. Packing foam comes in many shapes and sizes. It has a texture or pattern that makes an interesting design when printed. To pick up this fine texture, use printing ink rather than tempera paint. (Use printing ink you can wash off, not permanent ink.) You will need a cookie sheet or other flat surface for the ink and a special roller called a brayer to roll out the ink.

1 Packing foam is a soft plastic. Use your fingernails to cut away the areas that should not print. Remember that any area that is raised will be the area that picks up the ink. And when pressed on the paper, it is the area that will print.

2 Squeeze some ink out of the tube onto the cookie sheet. Use the brayer to spread the ink into a smooth, even layer.

4 Press the ink-covered foam block onto the paper.

3 To evenly coat the packing foam, press the foam block firmly into the layer of ink. You can press different sides of the foam block into different colors if you do not have a lot of blocks.

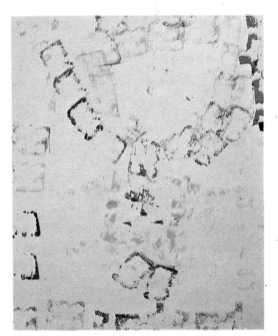

The design is the result of both the cut-away areas (they are white because they do not get any ink) and the raised areas (they are colored because they pick up the ink). The colored areas have a bubbly appearance from the texture of the foam.

Treasure boxes

To make a special box to hold all your treasures, take an old shoe box and cover the bottom with white paper, as if you were wrapping a present. Use glue or tape to hold the paper on the inside. Cover the top of the box in the same way.

To make the printing blocks, you will need white glue, printer's ink, and cardboard from old boxes, egg cartons, and paper-towel tubes.

2 Glue this cardboard shape onto a flat piece of cardboard with white glue. Hold it in place for a few minutes until the glue dries.

1 Cut out an interesting shape from the cardboard. Joel is cutting several circles from an egg carton.

3 Roll out some ink. Press the cardboard block into the ink and then onto the paper-covered box.

These colorful boxes are a great place to keep all your treasures. To make his treasure box even more personal, Joel used his hand as a block, pressing it into the ink and forming a handprint, shown on the box at right.

Lunch bags

If you take your lunch to school every day, you may want to have a special set of lunch bags. To make them, you will need brown paper lunch bags, cardboard, glue, and ink. You make the cardboard blocks the same way you made the blocks for the treasure boxes.

1 Cut out the shapes that you want to print with the cardboard. Michael is cutting out a star.

9

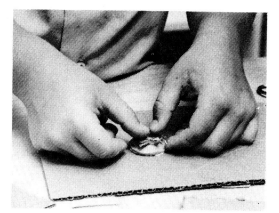

2 Glue a small piece of cardboard to a large piece. Then glue your shape on top of the small piece. This raises the shape so it is the only part of the block that picks up the ink. Press the pieces together until the glue dries.

3 Coat the cardboard block with the ink, then press it onto the paper bag.

What a delicious way to carry your lunch to school or to bring food on a picnic. A block-printed bag looks so pretty you could use it to hold a present rather than using gift-wrapping.

Postcards

To make postcards, you need oak tag, which is a heavyweight paper, or an old file folder. With a ruler and pencil, mark off 4¼-x-6-in. (10.7-x-15.2-cm) rectangles. Then cut out the rectangles. On one side of each card, draw a line down the middle, so you get two 3-x-4¼-in. (7.6-x-10.7-cm) halves. One half is for the address; the other is for the message. On the right side draw three parallel lines for the address. Then draw a box in the upper right corner for the stamp. These lines on the back of the postcard are shown in the top photograph on the following page. The front of the postcard is decorated with string printing blocks, as described below.

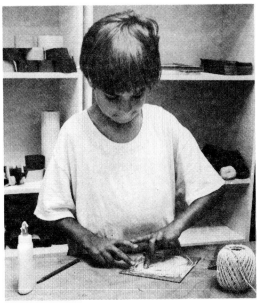

2 Wind a long piece of string around the glue-covered cardboard in the design you want. Then press the string to the cardboard so it sticks to the glue.

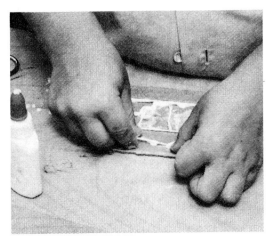

3 Or you can cut the string into small pieces and glue them to the cardboard one at a time. When the glue is dry, press the block into the ink and then onto the front of the postcard.

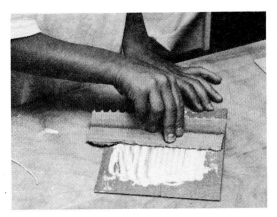

1 To make a printing block with string, spread white glue evenly across a flat piece of cardboard.

When you want to write a note to a friend, wish a happy birthday to your grandmother, or simply say hello to a favorite uncle, why not send your own printed postcards?

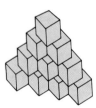

Notecards

Linoleum is usually used for floors, but it is an ideal material for printing blocks, because it is soft enough to cut but firm enough to print. The best linoleum to use is called battleship linoleum. It is available at hobby shops. To cut it, use special linoleum-cutting tools, such as the ones pictured on the following page. To make notecards, you will also need ink, a brayer, a cookie sheet, and paper. Start by making the notecard. Cut a sheet of paper to twice the size of the linoleum block. Then fold the paper in half. (You'll be printing only on the front of the card.)

1 Draw your design on the linoleum with a pencil. Then, using a cutting tool with a large blade, cut out the large areas that should not print. Always remember to cut away from yourself and to keep the hand holding the linoleum behind the blade.

4 Beth changes to a fine blade to cut the lines of texture in the basket.

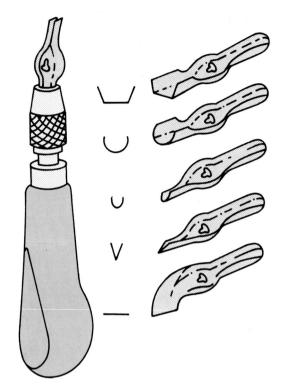

2 Linoleum-cutting tools usually come with one handle and several removable blades. Each blade cuts the linoleum in a different way. The cut each one makes is shown next to the blade, above.

3 Choose the blade that will cut out what you want. Above, Beth uses a medium blade to cut out the inside of a basket handle.

5 Leo makes a bold, abstract design by cutting into the linoleum in various directions, using a blade that makes a wide, thick cut.

7 Place the folded card on top of the block and go over it firmly with the back of a spoon. This will make the ink stick to the paper.

6 When you are pleased with the design on the linoleum block, put it aside. Roll out the ink on the cookie sheet until the brayer has an even layer of ink on it. Then roll the brayer over the linoleum block until the block is evenly covered with ink.

8 When the entire card has been rubbed with the spoon, carefully lift the paper off the block.

With linoleum blocks and a variety of cutting tools, a wide range of block-print designs are possible. The designs can be simple or complex, bold or delicate, abstract or realistic.

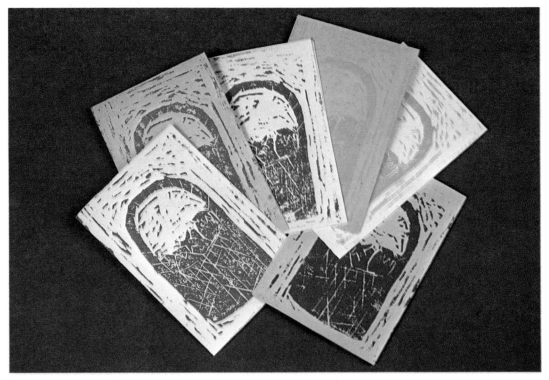

The same linoleum block can be used over and over again, on plain or colored paper. You can coat it with different color inks each time. Just remember to wipe off one color ink before applying another color.

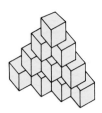

Wrapping paper

You can make wrapping paper for birthday gifts with the same type linoleum blocks you used for making the notecards. You may want to make a birthday card to match the wrapping paper. For printing, you will need white or colored tissue paper. Tissue paper is a thin, fragile paper. Handle it carefully so it does not tear.

Sarah places the inked block face down on the tissue paper. Then she presses down on it so the ink sticks to the paper. (If you try rubbing the paper with a spoon, the paper might tear.)

You can repeat the design of the linoleum block across the tissue paper in one color, or you can alternate colors as Sarah did. She printed the block in one color, leaving space between the designs. Then she printed the block in a second color in the blank spaces.

16

RUBBINGS

Making a rubbing is one way of reproducing the design on a wall, a plaque, or a manhole cover. To be able to pick up the design, you must use an object with a two-dimensional surface. The design can be raised, like the lettering on a plaque, or it can be carved into the surface.

To make a rubbing, you cover the object you want to copy with a piece of lightweight paper. Holding the paper securely, you go over it with a crayon. The raised parts of the object will leave an impression on the paper. Everywhere else, the paper will stay white.

Usually, rubbings are made from gravestones, brass designs in churches, commemorative plaques, and manhole covers. But you can make rubbings from anything with a textured surface. Baskets, lamp bases, a piece of screen, a tiled floor, and many other objects you have around the house are all suitable for these projects.

If you want to make rubbings from objects you already have, the only materials you need are lightweight paper and crayons. If you want to create your own objects, you will need heavy paper, such as oak tag.

Rubbings are extremely easy to make, but they can have a lot of variety. You can alter the crayon colors with watercolors. You can also make rubbings on cloth. In the projects on the following pages, rubbings are used for wall decorations, book covers, greeting cards, and scarves.

MATERIALS

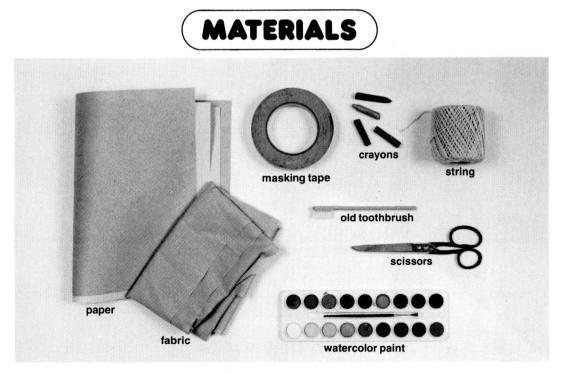

masking tape

crayons

string

old toothbrush

scissors

paper

fabric

watercolor paint

Texture rubbings

What kinds of things around the house have interesting textures that will show up in rubbings? You can start exploring textures in your house with some big areas, like wood floors, bathroom tiles, a rug, walls, and a radiator grill. Then look around for smaller items like pots and pans, baskets, a wastepaper can, books lined up on a shelf, and the telephone dial. To make the rubbings, select the items you want to use, and gather up some crayons and newsprint or other lightweight paper.

2 Place a piece of paper over the object you are going to copy. The bottom of a pie plate can have an interesting design.

1 Peel the wrappings from the crayons. In rubbings, you will use the side of the crayon, not the end you draw with.

3 Hold the paper securely, with one hand opened flat against it. Go over the

19

Book covers

Using a piece of ordinary string, you can create a rubbed design on paper and then make the paper into a book cover. You can use string, rope, crochet cotton, jute, or clothesline cord. Each kind of cord will create a different texture when it is rubbed. For this project, you will need colored construction paper, crayons, and the book you want to cover, in addition to the string.

4 If you are using an object, such as a small piece of aluminum screen, that is smaller than the piece of paper, position your hand on the paper so it holds the object, as well as the piece of paper, in place.

Sometimes an interesting texture doesn't give you a clue as to what the original item was. Dana used a rug, a pie plate, a piece of screen, a basket, a radiator cover, and a wood floor to produce the rubbing shown above. Could you have guessed what they were just from the picture?

1 Cut a piece of string to any length you want, and arrange it on the table in an interesting pattern.

2 Place a piece of construction paper over the string.

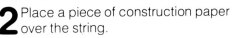

3 Use the side of a crayon to make the rubbing. You can go over just the string, or lightly rub the entire piece of paper.

4 Arrange the string in a different design. Place the paper back on the string, and go over it with a different color crayon.

5 To make a book cover, place your rubbing face-down on the table, and put the opened book on top of it. Crease the excess paper on top and bottom.

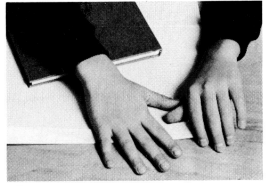

6 Take the book off and fold the paper along the creases you made.

7 Put the open book back on the rubbing, aligning it along the top and bottom folds. Fold the excess paper to form the front flap.

Susannah reads a book that is covered with a bright string-design rubbing.

8 Slip the front cover of the book into the flap that you just made.

9 Close the book so the cover fits around it. Then fold the excess paper for the back flap. Slip the back cover into the flap.

Leaf rubbings

You can make rubbings with crayons and then add more color with a watercolor wash. To add a watercolor wash, you put water on the rubbing and then go over the wet areas with some watercolor paint. This creates a very light coat of paint. The paint will not cover the crayon areas because the wax from the crayon protects the paper from the water.

For this project, you will need leaves, construction paper, some crayons, watercolors, brushes, and water. Try to gather as many different kinds of leaves as you can find, so you will have a variety of textures and shapes.

1 Arrange a variety of leaves on the table. Put the veined sides up so the veins will show in the rubbing.

2 Place a piece of construction paper over the leaves.

3 Holding the leaves under the paper in place with one hand, rub over them with the side of a crayon. You can use different colors for different leaves.

4 When you have finished the rubbing, remove the leaves. With a paintbrush, put water on the leaf shapes you are going to paint over.

5 Put a little paint on the brush, and go over the wet areas.

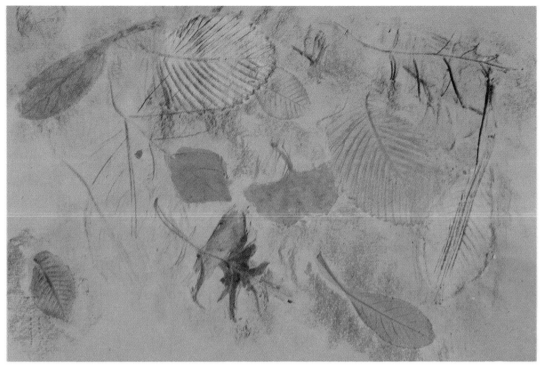

Jackie was inspired by the colors of autumn leaves when she chose the crayons and the watercolors for her leaf rubbing.

Holiday cards

Any holiday becomes a little nicer when you send your greetings on a handmade card. To make cards out of rubbings, you will need oak tag or an old file folder, scissors, construction paper, and crayons. Cut the construction paper to twice the size of the card you want, then fold it in half. The rubbing will go on the front of the card.

1 On oak tag, or any heavy paper, draw the shapes you want to copy.

2 Cut out the shapes that you drew, using a pair of sharp scissors.

3 If you like, you can cut abstract shapes out of the oak tag, without drawing them at all.

4 Arrange the cutout shapes in whatever design you want, putting them on the inside of the opened card.

5 Close the greeting card, being careful not to disturb the design you made.

7 Your fingers will cover part of each shape. To complete the rubbing, hold the shapes where you have already rubbed over them and go over the spots you missed. (If the shapes move as you shift your fingers, carefully reposition them.) When you finish the rubbing, remove the cutouts and add some detail with a crayon.

6 With one hand holding both the card and the shapes securely, go over the front of the card with the side of a crayon.

Whether it's a boat to wish someone a happy trip, hearts to sweeten Valentine's Day, or a pumpkin for Halloween, a handmade card is always nice to receive.

Manhole-cover rubbings

Any surface that has a raised design or a carved-out design can be covered with paper and rubbed. The surface can be a manhole cover, a gravestone, a plaque designating a landmark, a design carved on a building, a plaque explaining a statue, a design on a church or cathedral floor, or an old woodcut.

Many of these objects are not open to the public. If you want to make a rubbing of a gravestone, ask permission of the cemetery. If you want to make a rubbing of a design in a church, call to ask permission and find out what time it's best for you to work.

Some of the best surfaces for rubbings are found outdoors. They are often dirty. So, when you have chosen something to copy, use an old toothbrush or a stiff clean paintbrush to clean dirt out of the crevices. (Any dirt in the object will show up in the rubbing.)

One of the most interesting type rubbings you can make outdoors is a manhole-cover rubbing. To make one, you will need masking tape, crayons, and paper, such as newsprint or shelving paper, that is larger than the manhole.

1 To start, roll up four pieces of masking tape and put them around the manhole cover. (This cover is in the sidewalk. Never try using a manhole cover in the street unless the traffic has been blocked off.)

2 Smooth the paper, from the center out to the edges, and then press the paper to the masking tape at the edges.

3 Working from the center of the paper out to the edges, rub over it with the side of a crayon. You may want to have a friend work with you if the manhole cover is very large.

4 When you have gone over the entire cover with one color, use a different color on the areas you want to highlight.

5 In addition to manhole covers, you can make rubbings of plaques and other vertical objects. Simply attach a piece of paper to the object with masking tape.

6 Follow the steps given above to make the rubbing. But be sure you go over the words carefully, so you will be able to read them on the rubbing.

7 When you have finished rubbing, carefully pull the paper up from the masking tape. Then trim the edges for a nice finish.

This manhole-cover rubbing was made by going over the entire cover with red crayon. Blue crayon was rubbed lightly over some areas for additional color and texture.

Scarves

You can make rubbings on fabric as well as paper. To make a scarf, you need an 18-in. (45.7-cm) square of light-weight cotton, pinking shears (scissors that cut a zigzag edge), oak tag, scissors, crayons, pressing cloth, and an iron. Cut around the fabric with pinking shears. Edges cut this way will not fray, so you won't have to hem them.

2 Cut out the shapes, being careful to make clean, sharp edges.

1 Decide what shapes you want to use for the scarf, then draw them on oak tag. You need only one or two shapes. Make one pattern of each different shape.

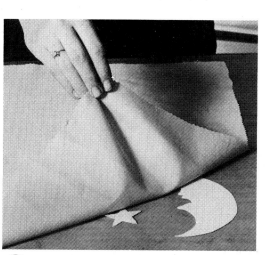

3 Arrange the shapes and cover them with the fabric.

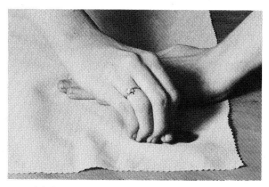

4 Holding both the fabric and the cutout shapes firmly with one hand, rub from your hand out toward the edge of the fabric. Fabric slips more than paper, so work carefully.

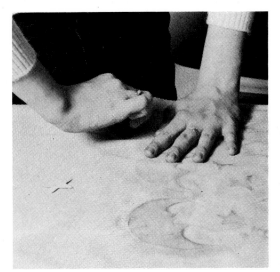

5 You can repeat the same shape as many times as you want. Beth used one moon and one star twice, then she flipped the moon so all the moons face the star.

7 Put the finished scarf on an ironing board, and place a damp pressing cloth on top of it.

6 Gabrielle cut out one intricate elephant for her design and rubbed it on the scarf in different colors.

8 Go over the cloth with a hot iron, being careful not to scorch the scarf. This will set the crayon colors into the fabric.

Gabrielle and Beth wear their rubbed-fabric scarves as head scarves, while Bryan and Leo wear them as neck scarves. The designs are visible either way.

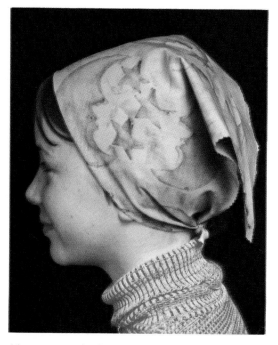

You can make beautiful designs, using only one or two shapes, by repeating the shapes around the scarf.

PAPERMAKING

Did you know that you can make paper at home? Can you imagine writing a letter to your grandfather, inviting your best friend to a party, or writing a poem to your mother on paper you have made?

Most of the paper used today is made from wood pulp, which is a soft, mushy mixture of wood fibers and water. Papers made from wood pulp include newspaper, homework paper, typing paper, paper towels, cardboard boxes, envelopes, and magazine pages. These papers can be broken down again with water and made into pulp in a food blender. The clean sheets of paper made from the pulp can be used for letters, party invitations, greeting cards, or drawings.

In addition to old paper, water, and a blender, you will need a sheetmaker. You can make one at home with three plastic dishpans. The top two dishpans have identical rectangles cut out of them. It is these rectangles that determine the size and shape of the paper sheets. The third dishpan is on the bottom; it catches the excess water. Directions for constructing the sheetmaker, for making several different kinds of recycled paper, and for making an envelope are on the following pages.

At the end of the chapter, you will also find instructions for making a paper decoration that looks like a stained-glass window and for creating marbelized paper.

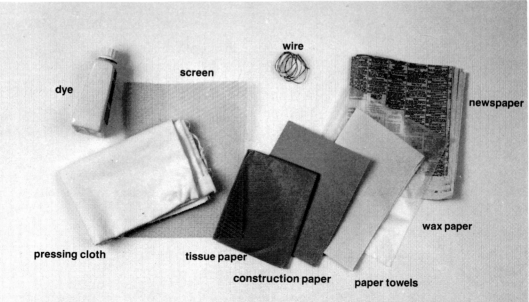

dye screen wire newspaper

pressing cloth tissue paper construction paper paper towels wax paper

To make a sheetmaker, you will need three standard size plastic dishpans; 6 ft. (1.82 m) of wood molding strips, ¾-in. (1.9-cm) wide by ¼-in. (.63-cm) thick; two pieces of aluminum screening, each 9 x 12 in. (22.8 x 30.4 cm); aluminum tacks; a ruler; a hammer; a handsaw; and a craft knife.

Making a sheetmaker is difficult, so get an adult to help you.

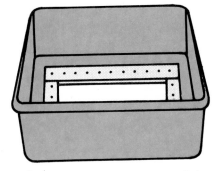

3 On the second dishpan, nail the wood strips to the inside of the dishpan.

1 On the bottom of one plastic dishpan, draw a 6-x-8-in. (15.2-x-20.3-cm.) rectangle. Cut out the rectangle. (Be careful; craft knives are sharp.) Cut out the same size rectangle from the second dishpan.

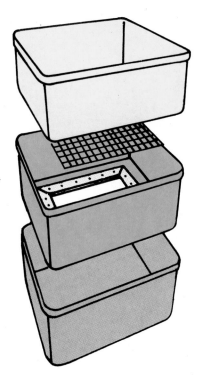

2 Working on the bottom of one dishpan, put four strips of wood around the rectangle. Hammer aluminum tacks through the wood to hold it in place.

4 To assemble the sheetmaker, put a piece of aluminum screening between the top two dishpans. Then set them inside the third dishpan.

Recycled paper

You can recycle any paper that is made mostly of wood pulp. Newspapers, old homework papers, paper towels, and used typing paper are examples. You will need half sheets of typing paper for one 6-x-8-in. (15.2-x-20.3-cm) piece of paper. You will also need a blender and water, the sheetmaker described above, and a pressing cloth and iron.

1 Remove all staples and tape from the paper. Also remove cellophane windows if you are using envelopes. Tear the paper into pieces about an inch square.

2 Fill the blender three-quarters full with water. Add about half the paper scraps. Cover the blender.

3 Turn the blender to a high speed and let it run until the paper is broken down into pulp. This takes just a few minutes.

4 Add the rest of the paper scraps and blend until all the paper has been broken down. Never uncover the blender or put your hands in while it is turned on.

5 Carefully pour the paper pulp into the sheetmaker. Don't dump it into the middle of the screen. Pour it so the pulp reaches all the corners.

6 Wait a few minutes to let most of the water drain through the screen. Meanwhile, put a pile of newspaper, covered by an old towel, near the dishpan. Now remove the top dishpan, and carefully lift out the screen.

7 Place the pulp-covered screen on the towel and cover it with another piece of screening. The towels and newspapers will absorb the excess water from the pulp; the extra screening will hold it flat.

8 Use a large can as a rolling pin to squeeze out the excess water.

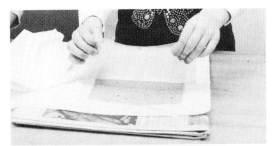

9 Remove the top screen and flip the bottom screen over onto a pressing cloth. Do this close to one edge of the cloth, so you have enough cloth left over to totally cover the pulp. Peel the screen off the paper, being careful not to tear it.

Natural paper

You can add leaves and pine needles to handmade paper for an interesting effect. The leaves can be fresh, green ones from a tree in summer, or they can be the gold and red ones that have fallen to the ground in autumn. You can use only one type of leaf or mix many different kinds of leaves in one piece of paper. You will need two paper towels for each piece of paper. The colors of the leaves will show up best if the paper towels are white.

10 Fold the pressing cloth over the wet paper and go over it with a hot iron. Press it until the paper is almost dry. Then put a weight, such as a heavy book, on top of the paper and allow it to continue drying overnight.

These recycled papers were made (from left to right) of old newspapers, blue typing paper, old homework papers, a yellow letter, and pink typing paper. The flecks of black are bits of ink that do not dissolve but are chopped up in the blender.

1 Tear the paper towels into inch square pieces. Also tear the leaves into small pieces and separate the pine needles from the branch if they are on one.

2 Fill the blender three-quarters full with water. Add half the paper-towel scraps and blend. Then add the rest of the paper-towel scraps and blend until the paper is broken down. Add the leaves or pine needles last. The longer you blend the leaves, the smaller the pieces will be.

4 Wait a few minutes until most of the water drains through the screen into the bottom dishpan. Then lift off the top dishpan.

3 Slowly pour the mixture into the sheet-maker, making sure that it fills the corners of the screen.

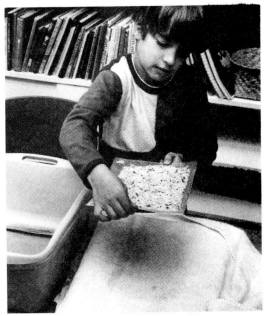

5 To drain the water from the pulp, put an old towel on top of a stack of news-papers. Carefully lift out the pulp-covered screen and put it on the towel.

6 Put another piece of screening on top of the pulp and roll out the excess water with an empty juice can.

8 Fold the pressing cloth over the wet paper. Press it with a hot iron until the paper is dry to the touch. Place a weight such as a heavy book on the paper, and let it dry overnight.

7 Lift the top screen off, then flip the bottom screen over onto a pressing cloth. Peel the screen off the set paper, being careful not to tear the paper.

Added to these handmade papers were yellow oak leaves (top), pine needles broken up only slightly by the blender (center), and green maple leaves chopped very fine (bottom).

Your imprint

You can put your imprint on a piece of handmade paper by adding a watermark. To make a watermark, which is a translucent pattern in the paper, you bend a piece of thin copper wire into the shape you want, and attach it to the screen with nylon thread. While the paper dries on the screen, the wire shape makes an impression in it. The impression can be seen more clearly if the paper is dyed. For this, you will need liquid fabric dye.

2 Sew the wire shape to the sheetmaker screen, using nylon thread.

1 Take a length of copper wire and bend it into the shape you want. Do not cross the wire. A double thickness of wire will make a hole in the paper. Cut off any excess wire.

3 Mix the paper scraps and water in the blender. You can use a mixture of old homework papers, used typing paper, paper towels, and some newspaper. Make up the batch in halves, following the mixing instructions given in the previous projects.

4 When the paper is broken down, add the fabric dye. Start with a few drops. Cover the blender and mix. Keep adding dye until the paper is the color you want.

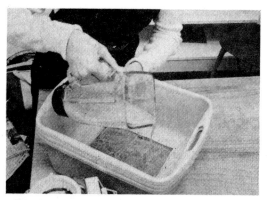

5 Carefully pour the mixture into the sheetmaker, making sure the pulp covers the wire shape. Let the water drain from the screen.

6 Place the pulp-covered screen on top of towel-covered newspaper, and put another piece of screening on top. Use a juice can to roll out the excess water.

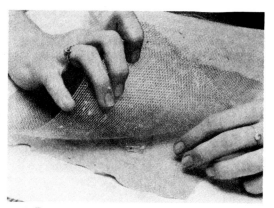

7 Remove the top screen. Flip the bottom screen over onto a pressing cloth. Peel the screen from the wet paper, being careful not to tear the paper around the watermark.

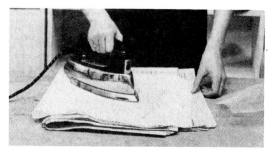

8 Fold the pressing cloth over the paper. Go over it with a hot iron until the paper is almost dry. Then put a heavy book on top of the paper overnight.

Bryan made his initial for a watermark. In this close-up view, you can see how the paper picks up the pattern of the screen it was made on.

Fabric dye was added in varying amounts as these papers were being made, resulting in paper that ranges from pale to deep aqua. If you look very closely, you can see two water-marks. The paper on the right has a snail shape and the dark paper has a B.

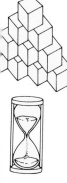

Matching envelope

If you want to use your handmade paper for an important letter, you can make an envelope for it. You will need white glue and a square piece of construction paper that is about one and a half times as long as the longer masurement of your paper. For example, to make an envelope for a 6-x-8-in. (15.2-x-20.3-cm) letter, you will need a 12-in. (30.4-cm) square of paper.

1 To make a square from a rectangle, fold the shorter side of the paper over to the long side. Cut off the excess.

2 With one corner of the square pointing away from you, place the letter in the center of the square. Fold the sides over as shown, leaving enough space for the letter to be slipped in and out.

3 To make notches in the envelope, make ½-in. (1.2-cm) slits along the fold lines on the top and bottom of both sides. Then cut in from the sides to meet these cut lines. Remove the small triangles of paper.

4 Fold the side flaps in. Then fold the bottom flap up, making a straight fold that runs from the point of one side notch to the point of the other.

5 Trim off the part of the bottom flap that extends above the side flaps.

6 Put a thin line of glue on the side edges of the bottom flap. Fold up the flap and hold it against the side flaps for a few minutes until the glue dries.

Whether you want to write to a faraway friend or send an invitation, handmade paper and a matching envelope will make the message special.

Stained-glass paper

Have you ever admired the beautiful stained-glass windows in a cathedral? You can make window decorations that look like stained glass, using wax paper, colored tissue paper, and construction paper.

2 Arrange the shapes on a piece of wax paper. Don't put the tissue-paper pieces out to the edge of the wax paper. Use a piece of wax paper larger than you want your design to be.

1 Cut the tissue paper into small pieces. You can make squares, rectangles, circles, or irregular shapes.

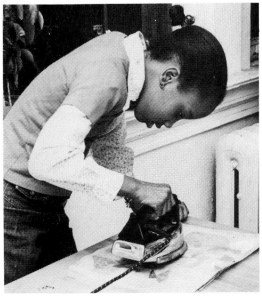

3 When you are pleased with the design, place another piece of wax paper on top of it. Go over the three layers with a low-temperature iron. Wax from the wax paper will melt and secure the tissue paper. Move the iron lightly over your design.

4 Trim away the extra wax paper on all four sides.

6 Cut the fold from the construction paper so the rim in back is the same width as the rim in front. (If the whole sheet of construction paper is glued to the back of the wax paper, it will prevent light from shining down through the design.)

5 You can make a frame for the stained-glass design by rimming all four sides with construction paper. To begin, fold a piece of construction paper over one edge of the wax paper, letting it overlap the front by 1 in. (2.5 cm). This overlap will be the front rim.

7 Put glue on the inside of the fold. Then slip the edge of the wax paper inside the fold and hold it in place until the glue dries. Frame the other three edges in the same way.

If you hang your framed stained-glass decoration in a window, the sun will shine through the colored tissue paper, making it look like the stained-glass windows in a cathedral.

Marbelized paper

Marbelized paper has swirled designs that resemble marble. It is a special type of decorated paper that is usually used on the inside cover of leather-bound books. To make marbelized paper, you will need oil paint; paint thinner, such as turpentine; disposable dishes for the paint; sticks for mixing; a plastic tub for the water; and paper.

1 Cover the table with newspaper to protect it. Squeeze some paint into the dish and add paint thinner. Mix until the paint is a thin liquid.

47

2 Fill the tub with water. Add the paint to the water. You can add more than one color if you like.

3 Stir the paint and water slightly with the stick. Water and oil do not mix so the paint will sit on the surface of the water in various patterns. You can change the patterns by moving the paint with the stick.

4 Place a piece of paper face-down on the top of the water. It will pick up paint in some areas. Where it touches the water, it will remain blank.

5 Quickly lift the paper by the edges and place it on newspaper until it dries. You can decorate several more pieces of paper until the paint is used up. Then add more thinned paint.

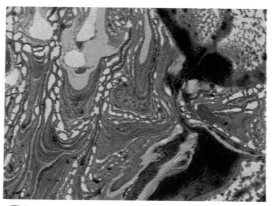

This design is just one of many resulting from red, yellow, and blue paint.